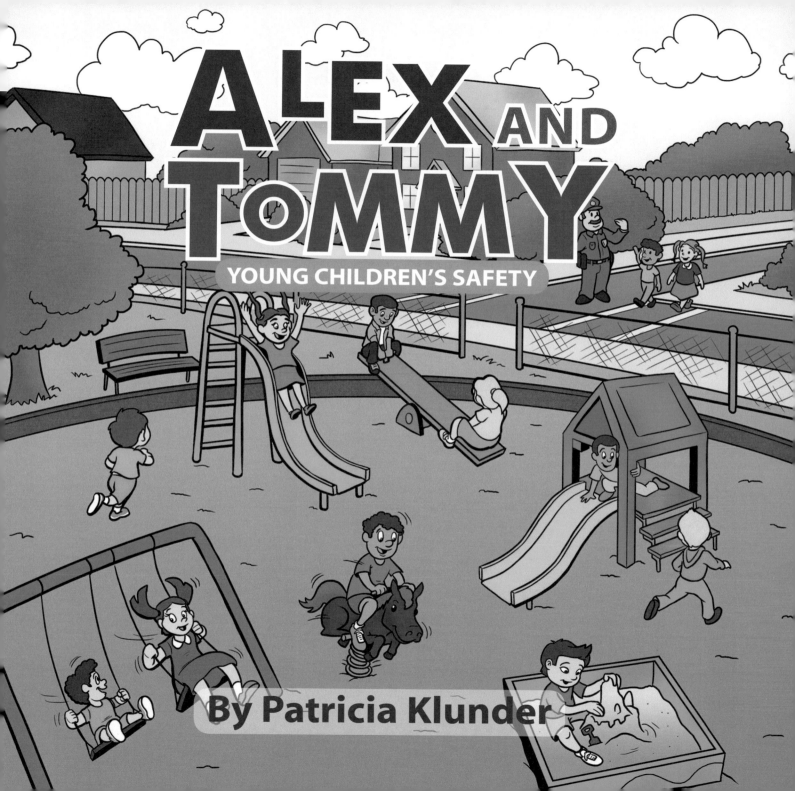

AuthorHouse™
1663 Liberty Drive
Bloomington, IN 47403
www.authorhouse.com
Phone: 833-262-8899

Because of the dynamic nature of the Internet, any web addresses or links contained in this book may have changed
since publication and may no longer be valid. The views expressed in this work are solely those of the author and do
not necessarily reflect the views of the publisher, and the publisher hereby disclaims any responsibility for them.

Any people depicted in stock imagery provided by Getty Images are models,
and such images are being used for illustrative purposes only.
Certain stock imagery © Getty Images.

This book is printed on acid-free paper.

ISBN: 978-1-4969-5558-6 (sc)
ISBN: 978-1-4969-5559-3 (e)

Library of Congress Control Number: 2014921176

Print information available on the last page.

Published by AuthorHouse 04/20/2022

authorHOUSE®

Once long ago in a very small town two boys were born. Their names were Alex and Tommy. They had a very kind mommy who took very good care of them. Alex was born four years before Tommy.

When Alex was born, she looked at him and thought he has the same cowlick as me. His hair was golden blonde and curly. Alex's large eyes were bright blue.

Mommy cradled her Alex in her arms, and started singing to him. ABCD EFGHIJKLMNOPQRSTUVWXY and Zed or Zee as it should be. Why do Canadians insist that the end of the alphabet be Zed? Zee rhymes with the alphabet. Mommy sang to Alex all the time. Alex never liked to sleep, because he always wanted to be close to his mommy. Once while Alex lay peacefully sleeping on Mommy's lap, she looked at him and shook, sigh she thought if I had too, I would absolutely die for you!

One day when Mommy was out shopping with Alex she realized that Alex was not by her side. Absolutely, terrified, Mommy ran from aisle to aisle searching for her two year old. Suddenly, she heard him gaily singing his ABC's. Mommy grabbed him and wrapped her arms around him. I love you so much NEVER EVER go with a stranger, please, because they might steal you! That's ok, Alex said, I was just looking for my cereal and was trying to help you.

Two years later, Tommy was born. Tommy was a wonderful baby as he loved to sleep. Mommy could even vacuum under his bed, and he would not wake up.

Mommy always read a safety book to Alex and Tommy every single night before bed.

Mommy taught them how to watch out when they crossed the street. Always look both ways she said. Ok Mommy I will always do that, said Alex. Tommy did not always listen to his big brother. However, Alex always took Tommy's hand when he looked like he was going to run across the street. Tommy some times did not like to have his hand held, and at times he struggled with his big brother. Leave me alone, he shouted, I can take care of myself.

Mommy said if you get lost, please look for a person with a badge who works in the store. Mommy always pointed out the nice workers in the store to them. DO NOT go with strangers, ever!! Ok, Mommy, Alex said. Ok, Mommy said Tommy I will always do that! So one day, Mommy, Tommy and Alex went shopping to a large new mall. They were looking for new school supplies. Neither Alex nor Tommy liked to go shopping. And all of a sudden Mommy noticed that Tommy was nowhere to be found. Frightened, scared, and terrified that her young son was lost, she ran and ran around looking for Tommy. Mommy started to cry, where is my son? Have you seen him she asked all the strangers in the mall? NO they said, what does he look like? He is blonde, two feet high has bright blue eyes, small ears, and he is wearing. Suddenly, a loud announcement came over the speakers, Would Mommy Adams, please come to the security booth. Mommy, who often got lost her self, could not find the security booth that fast. Finally Mommy found Tommy calmly eating an ice cream cone at the security booth. Tommy looked at Mommy and said what took you so long? Mommy looked upset so Tommy said do you want a lick of my cone? Mommy grabbed Tommy and wrapped her arms around him. I love you so much and I am so glad that you listened to my advice!

Mommy talked about mean men or women who sometimes want to touch your private parts. Mommy explained that no one ever is allowed to do that. She explained to Alex and Tommy that if it ever happens, to tell her, or a nice teacher, or even the police.

Ok, said Alex Ok, said Tommy, I will always do that!

Mommy also taught Alex and Tommy about electricity. Never, put anything but a strong electrical cord in an outlet. Never put a fork, spoon or anything in an electrical outlet. You might get a shock, Mommy explained, and that shock might kill you. OK, said Alex, Ok said Tommy. I will never do that! Mommy also taught Alex and Tommy about lightning storms. Never hide under a tree during a lightning storm! Always, lie flat on a beach if you are caught on the beach during a thunder and lightning storm! Ok, both sons said, I will always do that.

Mommy talked to Alex and Tommy about seat belts and always wearing a helmet while riding their bicycles.

Patricia A. Klunder

Do you want us to wear a seat belt and helmet while riding our bicycles? No, Mommy laughed and laughed and soon everyone was laughing, giggling and giving each other zerberts! Zerberts are blowing on your stomach until you make a sound that sounds like a wet fart! Ha ha ha Alex laughed hee hee hee giggled Tommy, as Alex gave Tommy another zerbert on his tummy! Mommy finally was able to stop laughing, although by then her stomach ached from laughing so hard! Helmets protect your head when riding a bicycle because if you fall off and hit your head the ground the helmet will protect your brain. Mommy said always wear a seat belt in motor vehicles! And all of the family, Mommy, Tommy and Alex always obeyed this rule.

Mommy Adams also chatted with her sons about wearing light colors at night so the cars can see you. Tommy suggested reflectors on their running shoes, to which Mommy said, great idea! When Alex was old enough to babysit his brother and other children in the neighbor hood, Mommy suggested taking a babysitting course. Alex said ok, if I can only make some money doing this. Of course, said Mommy if you are a good baby sitter, you can make a lot of money for little things like treats got yourself and your little brother. Alex took the baby sitting course and learned a lot of new things. He even taught his Mommy new things! Times have changed since you baby sat Mom he said.

Mommy said, much has changed since I was a child, she groaned with an old sigh. And of course sons please never open the door to strangers, and do not trust anyone until you completely know them! Even sometimes, when you think you can trust someone, they show their true personality and then you can't trust them. Trust and respect are so important with friends and family! Yes, both sons shouted, it is so very important!

Patricia A. Klunder

Mommy went on to chat about playground safety. Mommy was a nurse so she knew about playground injuries. Never stand in front of the swings, don't climb higher than you can handle on the monkey bars. Please don't slide down a slide unless you know that the slide is safe! Don't play with chemicals under the sink. Please don't put anything in your mouth, unless it is ok with Mommy. Alex and Tommy always made sure they did not do that. And please don't take pills or medicines unless you got it from me Mommy said, or a very trusted doctor!

We need to protect our planet, Mommy said to Alex and Tommy. Let's start reducing, reusing and recycling our old clothes. We can give our old clothes to the neighbours. And we can also reuse old toilet paper rolls for art projects. Mommy also said that she wouldn't run the car for a long time to warm it up. Good idea Alex and Tommy said. We want our polar bears to be happy in the North Pole where Santa lives with the Reindeer.

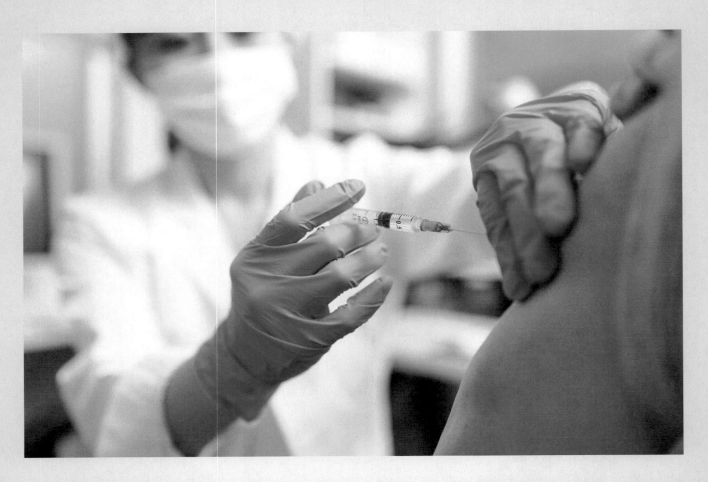

Mommy was a nurse and she truly believed in vaccinations. Please don't be afraid of needles and medicine they keep us healthy she said to both her boys. Ok, Alex and Tommy said bravely.

Life is worth living Mommy said to her boys. Please always remember that. If you or your friends feel sad, please let me know and I or a care provider can talk to them, to them feel better. Ok both boys said to their Mommy.

Always remember to protect yourselves from mean kids and adults. Mommy then decided to enroll both children in self-defense classes. Use your words instead of fighting please Mommy said. However, if they still won't leave you alone and hit you, defend yourself use your skills and don't be afraid.

Sometimes we get a little nervous Mommy said. Let's start relaxing by listening to pleasant music with instruments and birds singing.

Never start smoking cigarettes or it will be hard to stop Mommy said. Even if kids offer you a cigarette. Please say No! Ok, Alex and Tommy shouted.

Alex and Tommy were such wonderful children Mommy saw as they grew up. They trusted each other, played together and always loved each other very much. Sometimes Mommy Adams would cry tears of joy when Alex and Tommy did special things for her. Yes, they all loved each other very much.

Mommy breathed a sigh of relief one day, and realized that now even though both sons both lived so far away, their band of love was enormous! Yes, Mrs. Adams, said to herself, she had brought up the most amazing young men ever!

The End

Printed in the United States
by Baker & Taylor Publisher Services